virginiapope.com

'Huntin' Bill'

his

'ounds, 'osses, friends & foxes.

written and illustrated
by

Virginia Pope.

Published by
WITHE & WHORTLE

ISBN 0 9550816 0 2
ISBN 978 0 9550816 0 6

for

Sophie, Hugo, 'the cracker'
and You.

Foreword

'A strange and wonderful personal story told with great passion and beautifully illustrated.'

Robin Hanbury-Tenison

Chief Executive BFSS / Countryside Alliance 1995 – 1998.

The first book on Europeian hunting was written by Gaston Febus, Count of Foix, in 1387. Over the following six hundred years, thousands of books about hunting have been published, all of which had two things in common; They were all written in honour of the quarry and all written in the confident knowledge that hunting would always be part of rural Britain. After all, why on earth should something so beneficial to country communities, wildlife and through what used to called stewardship, the landscape ever be threatened? An Act of Parliament criminalizing hunting from the 18th February 2005 has opened a new era in the history of hunting literature and I am delighted that Virginia Pope has written one of the first.

Huntin' Bill is an enchanting book - essential bedtime reading, which will appeal to all ages. It very cleverly covers the unpalatable perspective of the Bill, not from the human point of view, but as seen through eyes of horse, hound and fox. These are anxious times for Star, Wisdom and Russet Brown. The first two potentially destined to be put down and the third, the Red Gentleman, to the snare, poison and the gun. Except of course, we care far too much for all three to allow it to happen. "Keep Hunting and Bollocks to Blair" is what I have been saying since this nonsense started and that, is precisely what we are going to do.

Contents

Contents

Hound Crier 18.03.2002

The early spring warmth slipped strangely away,
An icy mist rolled over hounds where they lay,
A darkness fell as in total eclipse
The spectoral hound curled back his pale lips.
The hounds they cow'd and one or two growled
A nervous young entry shook as he howled
An eerie bright light lit this blackened space
They saw and knew the huge hound's face.
Now they had to listen well
To all Hound Crier had to tell,
The eighteenth of March two thousand and two
He told them of that day, all that he knew
London, Westminster, Parliament, Ban,
Grasp the outcome of that if you can
On and on in a wailing song
It can't be right, it must be wrong
This time honoured sport of hundreds of years
An incredulous pack lay right back its ears –
Some hackles rigid, some teeth bared
Shivering, trembling they were suddenly scared.
As the news bludgeoned cruelly into their minds
Thoughts ran amock of their different kinds.
Bella, a beautiful black and tan bitch
Eyes big and round and nerves in a twitch,
'What of my youngsters, my show winning strain,
So sound of bone, so quick nose to brain?'
Bicester, her sister, full milk for her litter
'They'll never run fast or clamber the clitter
Nor even to go to a friendly walk
Stop that noise. Stop, stop this talk.'
Kindly, well named and liking a joke
A fair enough hound and so fond of folk –
What of the children patting at the meet?
What of the Kennelman, his pocket and the treat?
The Whipper-in, the Master, the farmer and his wife
The followers, field and Farrier, the Vet; people in his life?

Party envisaged jumble stalls, camaraderie, wild hunt balls
Interrupted suddenly by shuffling straw filled stalls
The horses, the other animals – he hadn't thought of that
The terriers no more barking at the wily teasing cat.
Poor defenceless laying hen, poor flightless fattening duck
Just a token left of them, a few feathers in the farmyard muck
The distraught ewes' lambs snatched straight from the birthing sack
Oh he didn't think he could ever dare to honestly look back.
Countryman, the lemon dog, who looked up when he ran
He wondered about his countryside after such a Ban
What was it, what was it that they wanted to do?
The very thing they longed to see would disappear from view.
Our countryside, our countryside that they longed to share
Oh why, oh why can't they trust it to our continuing good care?
The fabric, the fabric, don't rip it at the seams
For sure it will be torn apart and with it all our dreams.
Puzzle couldn't seem to figure out
What it all was really about
Something to do with a classless society
But we've always embraced a healthy variety.
A concert of different accents abound
When one is unseated or 'es 'it the ground
The coat is red, the coat is pink
It's not as silly as you may think.
When there's a cry of a view halloo
We need to see what the Huntsmen do
Rival thinks of the arguments noisy in the bars
The angry urbans mouthing "you yah yahs".
How can you reason when you don't understand
Come out for a season and learn about the land
We don't criticise or interfere with the way you live your life
Where is the pleasure in giving a minority so much strife?
The Hound Crier gone now, leaving feelings raw and deep
The owners, but one of these, fought with fitful sleep
Wisdom, the leader, the champion, the best

Laid his head on his paws and just settled for a rest.
What they can't get is how we honour our quarry
We love you Mr Freeman Fox but not your ways, so sorry
Your numbers must not too big grow
Your 'out of order' have to go
You have an ample larder but you insist on à la carte
Afraid for you my friend I am, some people aren't so smart
Bang! Bang! I may see the wrong end of a gun
What will be the end of you if all this is begun?
No more quick oblivion from just one your own size
What is in store for you will be cruel and not so wise
Poisoned, trapped or crippled certainly doesn't seem too kind
Lingering death at the hands of the seemingly deaf and blind.
A new day has dawned, the light filters through
Early morning chorus and a woo woo woo
Click goes the bolt on the kennel door
Kennelman stares at the shape on the floor.
"Oh Wisdom, Wisdom my dear old friend
Why, have you really come to your end?"
Hearing the sobs of the boy, all the hounds gather round
'Go forrard, we'll meet again in a happier hunting ground'.

*　　　*　　　*

Horses Tale

The rhythm of the countryside beats along with the four seasons
The steps of true countrymen are taken with good reasons
Early morn hear the horn autumnal equinox
Quiet meet, friends greet, rumble fit young fox
The men droned in tones and spoke with gravitas
Horses nuzzled muzzles and heard the word “impasse”
“Impasse?” said Star, “I’m past hearing about it it’s true
Do you realise it’s nigh on three years since the Hound Crier passed on through?”
“Really?” replied Cherry, with a bewildered sort of look,
(Cherry is named after a nearby babbling brook)
“I can’t seem to get a grasp of politics or its law
That I’d see you again I really couldn’t be sure.”
Warren the hunt horse, highly strung but very sweet,
Began, “It’s 24 / 7 at my place, news from the street
The proposed ban is proving difficult to beat
But ‘yes’ there will be a November opening meet.
Shortly after Armistice, oh please say extra prayers,
They gave their lives for freedom not a fox in snares,
The bill for the third time to go to the House of Lords,
After which Parliament might provoke hands to hilts of swords.
Anyone heard what happens to us?
Anyone give a tinker’s cuss?
I’m about all wound up and all out to sea
Do I belong to this guy or that Hunt Committee?
Too big for polo, too small to chase,
Too hot for most, I feel a disgrace;
Yet at this my work I really do excel
Don’t think I’d cope with redundancy too well,
You see this huntsman and I are the glove and the hand
We know intuitively where it’s at, the ‘lie of the land’.
I feel his thoughts travel down the reins,
I read his mind I know what pains,
What pains I know only too well
This threat that would mean a living hell.

Life at the Kennels sometimes gets too much
Not unlike a rabbit in a much too small a hutch
There's only one entrance now so he can see,
Who goes there, how, friend or enemy?
Everyone has to ring before they make a visit
Not our rural friendly way, now really is it.
So I don't know what will happen to him and I
It's probably a case or do or die,
Not so difficult over miles of rugged moor
Who's going to see if you step outside the law,
This country I gather is short on officers for crime
Well they can't be in all the places at the same time.
I do apologise you two I'm selfish and I'm rude
All the anger in the noise aloft makes me in a mood.
What of you Star do you know more than me?"
"Absolutely, if IT happens its off and over the sea –
HOT – stands for hunting ornithology taxation,
Hot foot to France for a life of less vexation
That's what the Master will keep on saying,
Ornithology I suppose is watching round hips swaying
So maybe a new life in pursuit of Wild Boar,
(That's what his missus calls him you should hear him roar!)
I am young and I am sound with a hunter's gene
One day I may have some foals to rear and to wean.
Of course being foreign there's different habits
They don't only enjoy the meat of rabbits"
Cherry's eyes grew dewy and rounder
"I've lost the point I'm beginning to flounder."
"Oh really" snorts Star "you're too soft by far
You belong in the age before the advent of the car"
"Well keep your mane and tail on," Cherry retorted
"If a horse could get on a high one it was Star when she snorted.
The pace of life on my farm may be slow
But you and I aren't that different you know
Today we're both lent out to VIPs from another pack,

See how you get on with a stranger on your back.
Mine's main interest is focused on the hound,
He will appreciate my sure footedness over stony ground.
Being hired out came about after the Foot and Mouth
As you know it was all around but virulent in the south,
All our sheep and cattle had to be destroyed,
A matter of income stated that we were differently employed.
The old farm buildings are changed to holiday homes
We're bound to the bank and living off their loans,
So three times a week this is what I do,
I really enjoy hunting like the rest of you do too.
If hunting's forbidden
Where'll I be ridden?
Nothings certain in life these times feel unsure,
Market? Market to basket? Basket props back your French
butcher's door."
"Oh cheer up" said Warren, "feel the oats warm in your veins,
Soon you'll hear the horn and we'll be off down the lanes."
Toot Toot, black leather boot pressure in the ribs,
Quick turn on the forehand in answer to his nibs.
A stream of healthy horses trot on from the meet,
Quite a boon to industry leather tack to well shod feet.
Hard to believe one breed of them may be wiped away,
Keep two for tourism. Rare breed. Pay to look. This way.

*　　　*　　　*

FOX COURT

I
Day Break

Day broke, Russet Brown pulled himself out of his earth deep in the wood that he called home, he drew in the clean frosted air, stretched his sinewy limbs as a cat might, shook and set off to break cover to the southern side. “Ack Ack Ack” Russet Brown tensed with irritation, ‘infernal Jay’ he thought ‘damnable down side to woodland dwelling.’ “Ack Ack” it continued “Look Look” “Fox Fox” “Court Court” ‘Quite possibly if you keep pointing out my whereabouts! How they know your every move and want to keep shouting about it beats me, surely not on account that we may disturb their odd cache of nuts and berries or beat them to the occasional fallen mouse or whatever? We don’t do them any real harm, not that given the chance I wouldn’t half love to divest one of his little buff jacket with its flashy blue wing patches, that would put a stop to the flitting around telling tales to the gunkeepers’ dogs and the hounds when they’re entered to our wood. How does he know there’s a court tomorrow? It is rare for foxes to gather together, usually a well kept secret on account of the added danger, who is his consort?’ A final “Ack Ack” as the fox squeezed under a rickety old gate and out into the open countryside – and one more shrill “Ack” “Oh p--- off to Pinewood,” growled Russet Brown “and fire yourself out of a gun.”

II
A Little Light Breakfast

In the very prime of his life, youth and vigour shining strong in the burnished coat, the fox effortlessly trotted up the heavy furrows of plough and without pausing pushed on over a wide expanse of steep pastureland until he reached the summit of the hill; he stood for a moment, before him lay the valley, the sleepy town and beyond the mountainous hills of the moorland, he could smell them all. The highest point was to be the meeting place, the place, where the foxes were to hold their court. 'Food first' thought Russet Brown, the dawn chorus he noted, had already subsided to a few chirrupy pleasantries whilst the birds were now more fully concentrating on their breakfasts. The frosted chill on the air had been chased off by the sun, it was hard to believe that it would be Christmas Day soon, fox courts were unheard of in December in olden times, the conditions of temperature versus larder would have made it impossible for many foxes to survive in the same place. Erring on the side of caution now the day was underway, Russet Brown trotted along nearer the hedgerow, stopping here and there to pick a few berries within his reach, even some ripened blackberries in sheltered places which earnt him a scattering of wild carrot florets that stuck impertinently to the end of his nose, this was distracting, he found an old cow pat near by, rubbed his hot body luxuriantly into it and moved his snout through the grass to dislodge the little white flowers, 'crazy' he thought, 'all this in winter, I shall ask Beaufox about it when I join him later, he is so wise.'

Lorries rumbled in the distance, the early risers, the farmers, greeted the morning with coughs and oaths, a pushing and shuddering of winter swollen doors, a 'Ho Ho' to the cattle, and a piercing whistle to the dogs, the fox and his keen hearing listened for the sound of opportunity, after all this is how he lived. Soon enough bleat of goat and rattle of pail met his ear, he followed the sounds down a stony track, slid past a little cottage and crept into Farmery Rose's yard, he pressed himself silently into the shadow of the barn door, there was Farmery Rose squatting on a log, too knobbly to split, too big to burn, bucket locked between arthritic knees, competent hands coaxing the last few drops of sweet smelling milk out of a nervy young nanny goat. Farmers generally have a cat or two about to keep the rat and mouse numbers down and after milking fill an old dish with the last drops in the bucket as wages. Farmery Rose's cat appeared in the doorway from routine, caught sight of Russet Brown, bristled her hairs and yowled like a banshee, the nervous nanny bleated her anxiety, leapt her fear, knocked the pail, tipping the milk and somehow getting the pail handle around her hind leg, which of course when she tried to run away ran away with her too nipping at her heels with much ringing and clattering.

What a farce in a field, nanny, bucket, billy and kids with Farmery Rose bringing up the rear screeching at the goat to calm down "you mad b----r" which seemed not surprisingly to have the opposite effect, out of sight the motley crew continued their noisy circus, and down another two fields; leisurely Russet Brown lapped up the still warm milk which obligingly had neatly run into a dip in the floor, the cat watched from the safety of a beam high in the ceiling, tail twitching in fury, the fox licked his tongue high over his lips, lifted his leg on the door jamb to add to the general fun and speculation, helped himself to an egg laid at random in the goats' hay and carried it off gently in his mouth to find the sunny side of a bank where he could sit down and enjoy it.

III
Fox About Town

Fresh egg and forty winks equals fortified fox, Russet Brown scratched behind his elbow thoughtfully and looked at the position of the watery sun which had reached its zenith and was beginning its decline for the day, he still had a long way to travel, there was nothing for it but to take the short cut through the town, he'd been through once before unscathed but he was unused to town living and the strangeness of it all jangled his nerves; he defecated on the bank's edge, then ran on at a steady pace the while thinking of the Bristol fox he had met not long since. Evidently he had helped out a friend during a run who was in danger from hounds, by taking his place, for he was tired; after distracting hounds for some miles found himself distracted by a hot little vixen and then another and finally ended up a long way from home; he had told him people were used to seeing foxes in the city, to just act normally. But where Russet Brown was headed was just a small market town where yes, people were used to seeing foxes but in the woods, and the fields, not in the streets; if he could keep his nerve, he'd take them by surprise, the human being is usually so taken with his own surprise that there is time to slip on by before he recovers his equilibrium and so it was by a close shave of the whiskers.

The high street was busy with humanity, the very smell of them and the fumes from the motors made Russet Brown's stomach curl, he thought of his appointment with Beaufox how he wouldn't, couldn't, let him down. "Breathe through your mouth, stupid fox, and occupy your mind with something else" he said to himself and "Thank you God for my sharp hearing, and my sense of smell, for the courage of a wolf, the feet of a cat. Thank you God for all of that. I pray to use them well. But why the white on the tail do tell, a dead giveaway like a collar with a bell. It's to test my courage I daresay, OK Town here comes Brown." With that the fox trotted up the High Street, a collie was tied to a post outside the newsagent. Tied up with leash and agitation, 'poor thing' thought Russet Brown 'that's cruel, he should be looking to some sheep on the hill, how lucky the fox is to be free'. The demented creature saw him and made spasmodic high pitched barks not knowing whether to raise the alarm or sit and be quiet as he had been told – the latter apparently as a bustling body came through the shop door and pulled the dog's collar tight and dared eye contact and threatened with rolled newspaper, this commotion had caught the attention of two pit bulls strutting their stuff with their leather and studded owners, the sheepdog's whining pitch tipped a switch in their brains they went for it and each other, oh glorious tangle of leads and legs, ladies, laughter and lambasting, perfect for the 'slip on through', the fox crossed at the pedestrian crossing, cars stopped in surprise, the fox was beginning to enjoy it all, foxes shouldn't or indeed any of us shouldn't 'count our chickens' – foxes frequently seem to be! A very young mother pushing a pram saw the fox and screamed loudly enough to frighten flight into gormless pavement pigeons. Russet Brown's brush touched her stocking free legs as he made a dash for it, she screamed even louder, now the whole town had their eyes on him. Pell mel he ran in and out of streets like weaving a hedge to complicate a chase, at last there were no more shops and just a few houses in rows at the edge of the town - Russet Brown was thirsty, he hopped over a small brick wall into a back garden looking for water – the tall grass was moving, nearby an empty guinea pig run, the fox watched the grasses like a cat watches her mouse then pounce, pounce and chop, the warm lifeless body easily gave up its pretty brindle pelt. The fox jumped back over the wall and made his quick silent way up the hill and away from the town.

IV
A Grave Business

The church clock struck three as Russet Brown looked around for his friend in the churchyard but where was he, he looked again and curled up at the head of grave fast asleep was Beaufox - Russet Brown lowered his head and tail in fawning respect to the older fox and chattered his teeth and whimpered but achieved no response, he nudged the old fellow who was laid up shadow side of the stone and was cold, Russet Brown nudged harder. The other fox opened one eye "Ah good, Russet Brown, I was waiting for you." "Well here I am Sir, please move from those long shadows let's get moving and get you warm again we have a mountain to climb." "Yes, my dear, we each have a mountain to climb, you must go and hold court and take my place. I hope the others will have the good sense to see that – the Hound Crier is calling for me very soon, they need me there." With that a strange chill came about and a bright light burnt close and then far away. Russet Brown nudged Beaufox's body and found it to be but an empty shell. The Rectory cat growled for no apparent reason. Before he knew it Russet Brown found himself running on and on and on on the spongy moorland turf. "Stop Russet Brown stop you'll run yourself in to the ground" whined the Hound Crier "stay where you're of most value." The fox stopped and shook and looked around, "who said that, oh never mind", he took a long drink out of a delicious peaty ditch and crunched a beetle by the bole of a wind contorted Rowan – 'I've come a long way, I'm nearly there – aren't those the seven deadly things?' Before him an ancient hut circle with seven stones remaining upright – he had heard a tourist calling them the deadly things and what they each stood for, they were a favourite scenting place for the foxes before meetings, he would go over, I bet lust is the favourite, he smiled to himself, many friends and acquaintances had passed there with that day, he added his own scent and sniffed around the others and thought about foxes and the seven deadly things – Lust, yes, whenever possible, Pride, well yes and no, would depend what in, Covetousness, yes especially if being pursued by the foxhunters they found it nigh impossible to get you out of one. Anger, definitely, Gluttony sure, Envy well yes, another dog's vixen; Sloth, of course, we never clean house we just move house. In lighter spirits he brushed through the heather, loving the smell of it and the wildness all around him, one more hill to climb and yes silhouettes of many foxes around the rocks of the tor, one barked out "It's Brown, hi Brown, where's the Duke?" – "Gone with the Hound Crier" "Come on Brown we've a ripe piece of fallen mutton here to share", too tired from the day to take any yet, he lay down and fell into a safe sleep with his kin around him.

'…little buff jacket with its flashy blue wing patches'

'…and the huntsman sent for a second horse'

iv

V
Chewing The Fat and Making A Plan

The foxes chewed the fat, in actuality there was little of this to be found on the toothless mutton, but, the bones were flavoursome enough. On the other hand there was indeed a great deal to turn over since their last meeting.

Russet Brown stood apart from the crowd taking in the scene around him, he didn't think he'd ever seen so many foxes gathered together before, he cast his eyes around for familiar faces, the individuals, Brush, Sly, Rufous, Charlie, Ginge, Red, Ikey, Lord Fairfox heads together with Chalkie, Larder, burying a bone to improve its flavour, leaving an end sticking out of the ground so as he shouldn't forget where it was – bit of a waste of time really with all these foxes around and one or two openly watching and waiting, force of habit Russet Brown decided, oh and Viki, how beautiful she looked in the moonlight. The family groups by place names, yes, the drain foxes, the rocks foxes and the copse foxes and by alphabetical order Amory, Arden, Atherston, Boodle, Brockle and on and on, many taking and passing down human names to the next generation together with the tales of fine runs and foxy derring do along with them; originally and paradoxically that fashion of naming began with one fox over two hundred years ago, realising that despite any difficulties hunting with hounds after his kind may bring about, one man in making the sport popular had saved his dwindling ancient race Vulpes

Vulpes from extinction and so he named his fifth son Henry Duke. Russet Brown wasn't named from noblemen more for the colour of his coat, his tongue licked from glossy russet shoulder right down to the end of a fine black stockinged leg, not so much in self appraisal but rather more for to seek comfort, an overflow reaction to the escalating din around him. The din that was bound to ensue after the news that soon there would be no more foxhunting. The din, was an amalgamation of each in the assembly needing his say, each say sounding its own emotional chord on a steadily mounting scale. Russet Brown skirted stealthily around different groups exchanging opinions, not wishing to disturb them for he needed to glean those opinions if he was to try and take Beaufox's place he must try and follow his lead, he used to say there were many ways of looking at one thing and you should take into account another's opinion before coming to any firm conclusions. "Sheer bliss no more bothersome Tuesdays and Saturdays, oh to saunter through the week undisturbed, good riddance to 'em"

"Wonder what they'll do instead, they're bound to do something"

"Can't say I give a damn"

"Hounds?"

"On leads?" Snigger

“Or?”

”Could be or, after all there’d be no point in ‘em”

“Terriers?”

“Wouldn’t trust them to keep no laws s’not in their nature”

A group of young blades full of the exuberance of youth were fooling about and becoming helpless with laughter. “A ban on smoking in public places” they sang, “a ban on hunting with hounds. Poor old Homo sapiens he might as well go to ground.”

“BANtam” cackled one as he jerked about trying to look chicken like. So another went as to catch him.

“BANgkok“ added the next and two others set upon him, rolled him over and over down a slope until they all lay in a tangle at the bottom quite out of breath.

“At last” said a fine vixen a few barely discernible grey hairs around her muzzle “I shall no longer have to worry about my daughter living right on top of the Kennels, she will insist that she is quite free to come and go as she pleases where as it is the hounds that are kept safely behind bars, she just loves to be where its at as she puts it and no doubt her relaying pertinent news to us all has been a boon to foxkind, but you never know, and then there’s poor Chalkie I know the huntsman took him in when he was an orphan and raised him safely from predators, so hard on him with that ridiculous coat, something missing in his genes I daresay, it happens sometimes you know, I had a friend like it, dear Blanche, made her life a misery. Never could relax never made old bones – I think the huntsman was misguided, his hounds are pretty biddable, don't we know it, but he has to be seen to be doing his job, what is he going to do if some dim wit in the field holloas at the sight of Chalkie with hounds near I'd like to know and then of course Chalkie isn't properly wary of humans…and on she went, the couple of vixens she had cornered as audience had a glazed look in their eyes.

Food was the topic in one group "Well, there are no rich pickings where I live, I depend on the horse dung beetle for my staple diet so a diminished larder for me when hunt horses are taken out of the equation. I've been thinking lately especially when the weather is spiteful and the empty stomach aches, of moving on to where town is taking country and trying the urban life, a bin near to your earth with your daily requirements"

"Too many foxes close together too much mange"

"You starve to death with the mange"

"Yes, I've heard of foxes being so demented with it they eat off their own legs"

One or two shuddered involuntarily their eyes wide with apprehension, Russet Brown dipped in and changed the subject "Weren't the days when the countryside marched in the towns fabulous for food though?"

'Good move for morale, Russet Brown you're getting the hang of things' noted the fox who thought a lot but never said much and soon enough they were cheerfully reminiscing about days of most enjoyable pilferage. Preferences were shared over warm freshly taken chicken, duck and game, fresh or not so fresh eggs and carrion in general. One recalled the huge size and succulence of a hutched rabbit, they all agreed that wild rabbit wasn't very plentiful and not to touch the ones that didn't run or you would be very sick indeed.

The thinking fox withdrew from the group to think, 'man is an enigma to me he is supposed to have a high intelligence but really has barely the wit of a worm. The Coney is good to farm for his fur and his meat. They set him down in lands where no rabbit had lived before, the rabbit thrived, he had no natural predator there, he thrived too well and was claimed a pest, they set another rabbit down amongst them who carried a flea with the pox, and that act has caused terrible pain, man doesn't eat much rabbit meat now the sight of myxy rabbits offends his appetite..and in the same lands they have set down foxes and they are thriving….I wish I wasn't the thinking fox, thinking doesn't help. Mother Nature why can't they hear you?' He didn't notice the other foxes staring at his hunched shape or hear them remarking "he's off again" "it's those herbs he eats" "tisn't for a fox" "he's never right" "oh leave him alone he doesn't do any harm"

The youth were still joshing, one taunted "If you were edible, then there's a different matter, everyone would want to hunt you Mr Vulpes fines herbes you'd be one fox in real deep batter," and then with great agility made it to the top of the tor to gain supremacy over his snapping friend.

"Where do you get your news from Fairfox?" asked Chalkie "Well, from that young Viki at the kennels, a whippet called Tatler visits the hounds most weekends with her MFH, she shares a decent London garden with the City fox Franti during the week and the news filters through from there." "Can you tell me about the fox who was found in Port Cutlas House round about when Otis and his fellow men burst into Parliament in session, they say he was a bagman." "They, my dear fellow will say anything, pity was this impulsive chap went in when it was a bit quiet but he did put the wind up a couple of cleaners, you may imagine." Russet Brown hearing 'Otis' and catching sight of Viki talking to some friends, thought 'we'll call our eldest boy Ferry Fox he will have some daring and dash.' He began digging a hole to no purpose but felt better for it. “So the ban is around spawn to tadpole time?” “Yes about then, the hunters are looking into the validity of a law but my cronies think nothing will come of that.” “Do you think the ban is a good or a bad thing for you for foxes?” “For myself, well I've lived nearly all of my life now and wouldn't have had it any other way. I may not have the luck of the Duke and slide into that long sleep, a decent hound is something to be said for, for the grand finale, clean and quick not prolonged like a poor old snail at the thrush's anvil or starving starily into oblivion. As to the foxes in this country I confess I have my fears for them, being a quarry species may not look or sound perfect to some, but lifted above vermin status your breeding season is respected your habitat safeguarded your numbers controlled and your right to a sporting chance is upheld; fellows like myself have had what everyone wants, Freedom, there is too an illogical affection for us and if anyone would listen that's what they wouldn't hear.”

“Someone said hounds would chase the clean boot instead what does that mean?” The old fox explained, Sly was within earshot and moved closer, his face near cracked in half, grinning with the very idea of hounds chasing man.

“Or drag hunting, what is that?” again the elder provided the answer, “What would the scent be?” one or two more were gathered around now, “More than likely a piece of you” Sly enjoyed saying. "No stupid", everyone chorused "We wouldn't be hunted anymore," Sly barked with mirth "Oh yes we would, there's fox control for the farmers, two dogs to flush you out and someone waiting for you with a shotgun and then the old outlawed favourites will increase undercover, fancy trap and gangrene or poison and belly ache?"

"Oh shut up Sly" said Ikey moving around and squaring up to him, tension was mounting and things were getting out of hand. Russet Brown implored everyone to calm down, no one heard and involuntarily did the best thing he could have done, lay back his head and howled out all the hopelessness he felt inside him. When the howl had subsided he heard Fairfox still droning on, he apparently hadn't been aware of anything, 'he must be really deaf' thought Russet Brown. "I'll tell you Chalkie about a great run of our ancestors, they made hounds run twenty seven miles, have you ever heard of the Great Wood Run?" Someone shouted out rudely 'BORING'. Russet Brown shot them a piercing look that came deep from within, everyone fell silent, he faced them and challenged "OK then whose for giving our lot a good run for their money?"

VI
Ladies & Gentlemen Hold Onto Your Hats The Chase Is On

Everything was in place at the last legal meet of the foxhounds, crowds were gathered in support, horses and ponies freshly shod and feeling their breakfast oats, jockeys of various shapes and sizes trying to put a brave face on things, the huntsman uncharacteristically downing a dram or two, a pack of hounds any vague understanding of the occasion forgotten in a mounting impatience to get on with business as usual, some terriers yapping in a box strapped to the back of a quad bike and a scenting day that must have come down gift wrapped from Hound Crier himself.

Russet Brown was a few miles away and thought the action plan over while he waited for his turn in it, he couldn't think of anything that hadn't been covered, each knew what he had to do and contingency plans were in place, and some foxes would remain in their outlook positions throughout the day, ready to be consulted and to take and give messages; Viki, Hop, Chalkie, Fairfox and a few others had been chosen, the only one aggrieved was Chalkie, he didn't want to be sheltered from the dangers along with Russet Brown's heart's desire, the old, wounded and weak he would show them all one day, his chance would come.

Russet Brown, unbeknownst to Sly was just a little upwind from him. He had been put in a place as far as possible away from any railway track, he had led hounds to their death once before, there must be a sporting chance, Russet Brown didn't imagine Sly had been outfoxed by this placing however tactfully and attractively packaged, he didn't trust him not to think up something else underhand, Sly was aware of all this but he didn't know that he was marked, he thought Russet Brown to be at quite a different point on the map. They continued to wait. They both thought of Viki, Sly had heard of the great promiscuity in the town fox population, all living so near to one another how convenient, litters of cubs sharing two or three fathers, he thought he might introduce that into this sleepy part of the countryside, he wasn't put off by long distances, he'd wipe the smug look off that leader's mask who did he think he was, some of Viki's cubs would blatantly be his, he grinned lasciviously and admired his brush, no white on his tip he was dark all over inside and out.

Down in the village one of the masters rounded off a rallying speech by thanking the landlord of the Old Coaching Inn for the warmth of his hospitality, everyone applauded, the huntsman blew a couple of notes on his horn to signal the off and jogged up the high street hounds at his heels; this time honoured scene depicted on many a jigsaw puzzle was soon to have its pieces thrown in all directions, for as the huntsman rounded the corner at the top of the street his pack unbidden burst into song and, like football supporters busting a turnstile, all threw themselves at, on, into and over the lych gate, somehow getting the other side of it to scream down the path towards the Church. The whipper-in with great presence of mind and indeed agility, jumped from his saddle to the top of the churchyard wall and at great speed, top boots sliding over gravelled path, disappeared into the church porch and bang closed the heavy door, but the hounds were on a different line and took the other path out of the churchyard. Hot under the collar and red in the face the whip mumbled "Mornin" to the grave digger who was leaning on the handle of his spade, "see anything?" the gravedigger however was from the see all say nought academy, he simply spat on the palm of his hands rubbed them together grasped the spade and resumed his work.

The hounds ran straight into the grounds of the old Squire's house now a residential home, they paused to check on the lawns right in front of the house, the huntsman out of respect for the manicured grass, but cursing under his breath at the lost time, dismounted and looped his reins over a piece of park railing, he arrived at the same time as the residents who in their excitement hadn't stopped for hats, gloves or coats and were ignoring chastisements from a murderous looking matron and so woken from their now institutionalised existence were taken back to youth when they rode horses to

hounds before the war. A frail lady sat in her wheel chair, lace edged handkerchief held in the direction of the rose garden, the huntsman hat in hand went to enquire "Good morning madam, did you see exactly where...."

Before he had chance to finish or she reply three others came up all talking at once and all pointing in different directions. The huntsman thanked them so much and with the help of the whip rounded up the most of the hounds, on their way out he passed the bent diminutive figure of an old boy who was a true countryman, "there were four" he puffed out short of breath, "thank you Colonel" said the huntsman, he didn't dismiss it out of hand there was certainly something different going on today, he looked at the lane crammed with the jostling field all eyes were on him. 'Right' he thought 'let's away from here', he led the whole party off and up the hill at a spanking trot, he continued, he passed favourite places for entering hounds, he intended to put a good distance between himself and the village and sober up the hounds horses and riders with a bit of a work out, after the third hill all speculation and chattering had ceased, horses were concentrating on their work and the hounds biddable again ran along waiting for their orders.

Russet Brown quickly shook himself out of his reverie when he heard all the horses hooves hammering on the hard highway, ‘that was quick’ he thought, his eyes though remained trained on Sly, who was still sitting on the slope before him ‘get on with it’ he wanted to bark, just then the dark fox did get up, he stretched and slid down the bank onto the road straight past the gateway that was mapped out for him.

Russet Brown out of the corner of his left eye saw the first hound coming around the bend, his right ear picked up a rumbling lorry and the whine of a motor bike, he must act and fast, he placed himself in the middle of the lane waited for someone to see him and with a ‘tally ho’ from Huntin’ Bill confirming that, he slipped through the gateway marked for Sly, so here he was in an area of field fenced off for large white sows waiting to have their piglets. Sly had condescended to take this slot remarking how he would enjoy rolling in the pig muck confusing the scent, aggravating the pigs and hoping they would get nasty in their turn with the humans who may then also, but involuntarily, get to roll in the muck too. ‘Very clever Sly’ thought the running fox ‘when I steered you from the railroad line you immediately thought of the main road’. No more time to think about that, things were not going to plan, pigs ears make it difficult to see the small eye of the pig and what she may be thinking, easy or not one huge and angry pig was after him and at intervals around the outside of the pig netting hounds were marking him, with a burst of speed he didn't know he possessed the fox made for the wire and squeezed himself through, a searing pain in a front leg disorientated him for a moment, he had pulled a dew claw, then on he sped again, his leg numb, he couldn't feel the warm blood running from the tear, he ran down into a drain by the hedge and was about to give in, the hounds were so close, but from somewhere he swore he heard the voice of Viki, it urged him on, on down the drain through a small gap in the hedge, across the corner of the field, and into an open hay barn, it urged him to pull himself up and up the bales, he slid inbetween two at the top and lay there. Didn't Viki smell quite lovely, wasn't she the prettiest fox he'd ever seen, "lick the wound clean before you sleep, see you tomorrow" he licked and fell into a feverish sleep.

That Viki was actually there or not we shall never know, the hounds went close to the barn and then noses down ran over a couple of fields and on to a property where they were definitely not welcomed, they were called back and taken on again further out into wilder countryside.

Brush was a big framed fox, built for the longer run more than the sprint, he was enjoying jogging along laying his part of the trail, which he was doing with a deal of imagination, a little touch here a little touch there to discombobulate those in his wake and to buy him a bit of time later should he need it.

The weaving of this warp and waft began at a remote farmstead, its small oddly shaped fields divided by crumbling stone walls and beyond it the wilderness of the moors. Brush rolled in the good green goose muck that edged their pond to perhaps lighten the note of fox, he looked about in the cider apple orchard, the trees were old and bent, the branch of one growing along the ground, he ran up it and from there sprang like a cat on to the top of the moss topped wall just within his reach. Brush travelled along the wall until its end where it had fallen unrepaired into a heap, from there he crossed a ditch and paddled into the middle of a clear stream that ran from a spring up the hill and fed the duck pond on its way to the valley below; he followed the stream a good way and took cover under the over hanging lip of its side when he heard the farmer and his dog bringing the ewes down over the hill and home to have their lambs. Once they were safely out of the way, he was onto dry land and running through the heather, he ran on at a steady pace and then realised he was at the very boundary edge to the next door hunt, oh they were very territorial and so were their foxes, if he was to just run over the divide a little way, what fun, how they would all laugh about it tomorrow. Brush went over and further in than he meant to, he ran into two fit young dog foxes, they barred his way and bared their teeth, he was quite out of breath from his run, he tried to dodge out of their way but they kept encircling him and then all of a sudden they were gone and replaced by the hounds. The field kept a respectful distance, a lengthy final note came from the horn.

Everyone assumed they were heading for home now as they blindly followed the huntsman, for most of them were in unfamiliar territory, after a while they sensed by the set of the huntsman's back that he wasn't for turning and that they were headed away from home and hearth, small parties of them struck off in different directions hoping to find a wall or track to follow or recognise a landmark before the light began to fade. The horses were tired, the wind had changed direction, rain clouds were gathering overhead and it was getting very late. Hearths and homes, some hearths stayed quiet for the want of a match and some homes grew gloomy for want of a switch, dogs grew restless in baskets, cats whined to be let in cats whined to be let out, chickens started to put themselves to bed, children got hungry children got grumpy, husbands paced and let in doubts and jealousies and mothers were near out of their minds with worry as the time ticked on and the huntsman sent for a second horse.

VII
The Tally

"Viki said he got back at about midnight, the horse and the hounds took him home"

"Reckon"

"How did you get on?"

"Never had my turn"

"Nor did I"

"Sly?"

"Run over on the main road"

"Brush?"

"Bowled over"

"Chalkie"

"He's alright, in one of his moods though, bit preoccupied with something I'd say"

"Russet Brown?"

"Gone a clicketing!"

VIII
Saturday 19th February 2005

First pale light revealed an effigy of the Prime Minister swinging by the neck from the topmost branch of an ancient and immense beech, that seemed to stand sentinel with its peers along the roadside of a remote and wild piece of the English countryside. This the place steeped in folklore and legend about which tales of the terrifying are told; its tiny village to be the stage for all the local countryfolk to gather, to strengthen their unity, to show their support for their foxhounds who this day would be bidden to trail a dragged scent.

Nine am saw the car park full with police cars, the officers using their walkie talkies, grabbing a sandwich and putting padded body protectors under their uniforms: from north, south, east and west carloads of people converged on the meeting place, young and old 'some in rags some in tags and one in velvet gown', they took their places on either side of the road to form a warm welcoming committee of three thousand. Eleven fifteen saw a field behind the pub full with five collected hunts, two hundred horses and a pack of foxhounds. The hounds waited, bored but obedient except for one bitch who moved by a scent too joyous to overcome moved cautiously backwards through the pack the while watching the whipper-in and when he turned to raise his cap to the spokeswoman from the Countryside Alliance, made a hasty retreat through all the legs of the crowd who were strangely quiet, slipped through a gap in the hedge at the back of the field and disappeared from view.

The cheer leader, her podium the flat roof of the pub's porch, microphone in hand, thanked everyone for turning up to show their support and urged that they should do this the following Saturday, the one after and the one after that, faces were uplifted towards her as she spoke or watching two surveillance helicopters encircling the scene from above. At a leisurely pace up the middle of the road flanked by people for nigh on a mile trotted a white fox.

Hand held children watched the fox with indifference, in a landscape where hub caps, hocks, hounds and human knees are spinning past you nothing is that surprising. Dogs on leads reacted, some lunged forward hackles up, some shot backwards hackles up and the terrier puppy whose entry into this particular bit of real world was just too much, simply peed. The people who saw, weren't saying, they weren't nudging their neighbour and pointing in case there was nothing there, it would of course come out later, much ale would tell the tale, it would be told and retold and embellished and enriched and take its place alongside the other stories. They'll say it came from an earth in Wishtman's Wood.

Gradually the crowds dispersed, a few policemen helped to maintain the flow of traffic, the others looked relaxed as they shrugged off padded vests. A grimy old van housing a handful of sabs driven with aggression rattled past, it seemed no-one remaining took any notice of it, family and farming news was shared, a sprinkling of gossip added, then fond farewells and on with the day.

A little way up the valley an artist closed her studio door on a finished piece of work, reaching for coat and camera she went out to embrace the clean cold air and open spaces: a clump of reed trapped in a puddle of ice caught her attention, she hunkered down to look at the half moon print a bullock had cracked into the side of it, in the distance white tumbling shapes slid past the corner of her eye, she fully lengthened the camera lens and with delight watched the affectionate and playful reunion of hound and fox – the shutter lay idle.

Acknowledgements

First and foremost, heartfelt thanks to my daughter Sophie without whose unlimited help poor old Bill would have had to stay at home.

Thanks too to Sir Johnny Scott and Mr Robin Hanbury-Tenison for the generous giving of their time.

To all the splendid unwilling models, two legged and four, not forgetting my dachshunds collectively known as 'the mice' who never leave my side during artistic endeavours when in truth they would much prefer to be getting on with their own work.

Ginnie

Parliament ~ Lords

First published in Great Britain by Withe & Whortle

2005

Printed and bound by Antony Rowe Limited, Bumper's Farm Industrial Estate, Chippenham, Wiltshire SN14 6LH
(01249) 659705

FIRST EDITION

Distributed by the Publishers
Withe & Whortle
withe&whortle@dornaford.freeserve.co.uk

ISBN 0 9550816 0 2
ISBN 978 0 9550816 0 6

'an enchanting book - essential bedtime reading, which will appeal to all ages. 18th February 2005 has opened a new era in the history of hunting literature and I am delighted that Virginia Pope has written one of the first.'

Johnny Scott

'....told with great passion and beautifully illustrated.'

Robin Hanbury-Tenison

Huntin' Bill his 'ounds, 'osses, friends and foxes. Their tales 2002 – 2005 in verse and prose with pen & ink sketches and four colour plates. Illustrated by the author..

Photograph of the author by Sophie Price

ISBN 0-955-0816-0-2

9780955081606

WW

£10.00

ISBN 0 9550816 0 2
ISBN 978 0 9550816 0 6